Where Is Daddy?

Where Is Daddy?

The Story of a Divorce

by Beth Goff

Illustrated by Susan Perl

Beacon Press : *Boston*

"This story first appeared in the New York Times
magazine of May 12, 1969"

Text Copyright © 1969 by Beth Goff
Illustrations Copyright © 1969 by Susan Perl

First published as a Beacon Paperback in 1985
Beacon Press books are published under the auspices
of the Unitarian Universalist Association of
Congregations in North America,
25 Beacon Street, Boston, Massachusetts 02108
Published simultaneously in Canada by
Fitzhenry and Whiteside Limited, Toronto

Printed in the United States of America
(paperback) 9 8 7 6 5 4 3 2 1
Library of Congress catalog card number: 69–14608

ISBN 0-8070-2305-1 (pbk.)

Where Is Daddy?

Once there was a little girl called Janeydear.

She lived in a house with her daddy and mommy and a dog named Funny. Her daddy named the dog Funny, because that's what he was. And her daddy called Jane Janeydear, because that's what *she* was.

3

Daddy and Mommy both loved Janeydear very much. Sometimes Daddy played with Janeydear and Funny, and they laughed a lot. Sometimes, though, he didn't want to play, and he'd be angry at Janey if she made too much noise. Then Janey would be angry at *him*.

Mommy said Daddy only scolded because he had headaches and didn't feel well. Janey guessed she knew about that, because sometimes she had colds and felt bad, too. But it was always disappointing when Daddy didn't want to play.

One morning Funny was eating breakfast from his bowl on the kitchen floor while Janey was eating hers at the kitchen table. Mommy was frying pancakes.

"Where's Daddy?" Janey asked.

Mommy didn't answer.

"Is he still asleep?" Janey asked.

After a minute, Mommy said, "Daddy——isn't here."

"When will he be back?"

Mommy went to the sink and turned the water on. The water sprayed out as it came down, and it looked white.

"White water!" Janey said. "Like the edges of waves!" Then she remembered about Daddy. "When is Daddy coming home?"

"I don't know," Mommy said.

6

Janey got a sudden full-up feeling in her stomach and didn't want any more pancakes. She slid off her chair and sat down on the floor beside Funny.

"You and Funny and I will be keeping house for a while," Mommy said. Janey didn't say anything.

Daddy didn't come home for days and days.
Janey felt lonesome for him. Mommy was nice
most of the time, but she didn't want to play. Only
Funny was fun. Janey wondered if Daddy stayed
away because he was angry at her.

But then he did come, and Janey was so glad to
see him! He took her to the beach. Not Mommy,
not Funny, just Janeydear.

They played in the white water where the waves
ended, and sat in the sand and made a sand house.
And then they picked up a million seashells, and
Daddy wrote Janey's name with shells on the sand,
like this: JANEYDEAR.

"Write your name!" Janey said, and he did, like
this: DADDY.

"Now Mommy's name!" Janey said, but he didn't. Janey said, "Go on, Daddy, write Mommy's name!"

Daddy said, "Janeydear, Mommy and I are going to get a divorce."

Janey asked, "What's that?" She knew from the way he said it, it wasn't something nice.

Daddy tried to explain, but it was hard for Janey to listen. She was watching the waves, one after another, never quite the same. "Why does the water turn white?" she asked.

"Oh, never mind!" Daddy sounded cross. "It's time to go home."

When they got home, Daddy came into the house. Janey wanted to keep him there, so she tried to sit on his lap every minute. When Mommy said she had to go to bed, Janey said No! and made a great fuss. Then Mommy and Daddy began yelling at each other, and Janey howled at the top of her lungs because she was sorry she'd made a fuss and she didn't want them to yell like that.

When they put her in bed and went downstairs, Janey could still hear her mommy's and daddy's voices going up and down, sometimes soft, sometimes shouty. The anger between them made a pain inside her, and she cried and cried.

After a long, long time, Daddy came in and he stood by her bed saying "Janeydear, Janeydear," until she stopped crying. Then he said, "I'll always be your daddy just the same." He sounded nice, and Janeydear was very, very sleepy, so she went to sleep.

Next morning Mommy said the same thing, "Daddy will always be your daddy." But he wasn't there. He'd gone away again. Mommy said, "You and Funny and I will go to live with Grandma." Janey didn't say anything, and Mommy asked, "You like Grandma, don't you?" "I guess so," Janey said.

Janey liked Grandma most of the time, but she didn't like Grandma's house. Nobody ever wanted to play except Funny, and Funny wished they were in their real house, too. Grandma tried to keep Funny outside. This made both Janey and her dog unhappy, and Janey cried and yelled at Grandma, and Grandma said she was a bad girl.

Whenever Janey asked Mommy when they
could go home, Mommy didn't answer. Sometimes Janey yelled at Mommy because it made her
mad not to know when they could go home. It
made her mad that Daddy went away. Janey knew
it was bad to yell so much, but she just couldn't
help it.

Something else changed. Mommy got a job and was gone all day, like Daddy used to be. A great big fear grew inside of Janey — she was afraid her mommy would go away for all the time, like Daddy had. So Janey begged Mommy not to leave. Mommy promised she would come home every night. But Grandma said Mommy would not want to come home at all if Janey was so bad and angry and cried so much.

Janey remembered that she'd been angry at Daddy sometimes before he went away. She used to get mad at him when he didn't want to play.

Janey decided it must be very, very bad to be angry, because terrible things happened. She knew she must never say anything angry again, never ever.

And so she said hardly anything at all, because if she did talk even a little, some angriness might leak out and then Mommy would go away forever.

Mommy said, "Janey, you used to be my chatterbox! What's the matter, darling?" But Janey didn't tell her.

Grandma said, "She must be coming down with something!" So Mommy took Janey to the doctor, but he couldn't find what was wrong.

Janey didn't even fuss when Grandma chased Funny out of the house.

One day Janey went out to talk to Funny, but
Funny wasn't there. Janey called him twice, three
times, seven times. Finally Funny came. All of a
sudden Janey was mad at Funny—she was so mad
that she hit him and hit him. Funny yelped and ran
away. Janey sat down hard on the ground. She had
hurt Funny and she felt bad about it and glad about
it, both at the same time.

"Janey!" It was Mommy. She had seen what Janey did. Janey thought she would scold, but Mommy just said in a puzzled way, "Funny loves you, and you hit him!"

Janey yelled, "He went away like you and Daddy and I hate him!"

Mommy sat right down on the ground beside Janey and hugged her until Janey was quiet.

The next day Mommy asked, "Janey, would you like to come downtown and see where Mommy works?"

"Yes," Janey said, so that's what happened. Grandma and Janey went to Mommy's office, and Janey played with Mommy's typewriter, and said hello to some people, and saw where Mommy hung her coat and kept her papers. Then Grandma and Janey went home.

And Grandma said, "I guess it isn't much fun
for you here, Janey. Come sit on Grandma's lap—
I'll read you a story." Janey listened hard. When
the story was over she said, "Read it again, Grandma!" and Grandma did.

And every morning when she went to work, Mommy said, "Janeydear, remember, I'm coming back home tonight. I'm never going to stay away, never, ever." And she always did come home.

And Grandma began to be nicer to Funny, and she let him in the house sometimes. She even said he was quite a good dog.

And when Janey asked about him, Mommy talked about Daddy. She explained that there were lots and lots of reasons why Daddy went away, but none of them was Janey's fault. Mommy said Janey was a good girl, she was Janeydear, so Daddy certainly didn't leave because she was bad. Daddy would come to see Janey whenever he possibly could, Mommy said.

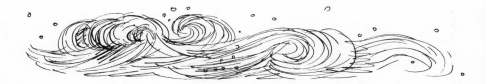

And pretty soon Daddy did come, and Janey was so glad to see him! They went to the zoo. This time Janey knew that Daddy would go away again, but it was fun to be at the zoo. Janey held tight to Daddy's hand, and they watched the seals splashing in the water. Janey asked, "Why does the water turn white?" And Daddy looked at her and said, "Bubbles, Janeydear. The seals splash air into the water, and it makes tiny little bubbles."

"Oh," Janey said, "bubbles! Bubbles, bubbles, bubbles!" And she laughed and laughed, and Daddy laughed too.

Janeydear felt much better.

Divorce is a very nearly intolerable concept for preschoolers. They have no words for the grief, confusion and loneliness it causes them. All they know is that their parents no longer live together and that the foundations of their world have split.

This touching story is psychologically sound. The names Janeydear and Funny set an atmosphere of love and reassurance and the story provides a structure in which an overwhelming puzzling event can be broken down to manageable size (like Daddy's anger, which is encapsulated and thus not so frightening). Beth Goff has captured the happenings and feelings that are common in the lives of children of divorce — the sudden change in surroundings, people, attitudes; the sudden intense fear of abandonment when mother goes to work; the turning to and turning against a loved pet (or person), and the need to control and hurt the pet just as the child has been hurt. This story may help children to stand off from their own confusing situation and identify with other children and then go back to examine their own feelings.

No one would argue that this story would provide children with a solution in itself. While it may be useful to provide a mirror through which people can see their own problems, they must be ready to examine them, and this point of readiness during the divorce experience varies among families, and must be assessed individually. At the same time, they must reach a point when the various family members are no longer mainly preoccupied with attempting to fix blame on each other. It is at this time that a story such as this one about Janeydear can be most helpful to all involved.

Why do we feel so strongly about Janeydear? Possibly because she reflects our old childhood fears of being helpless and lonely. It is important for parents who are divorcing to recognize these fears in themselves and their children. Parents' capacity for empathy with their small son or daughter can become blocked by their own personal distress at the time of the divorce. And the children's ability to confide feelings to their parents may become blocked, too. The main task, then, is to get parents and children back in tune with each other so that the parents understand what their children are feeling and can make their decisions on this basis. Perhaps a story such as this can serve as a bridge, helping parents and children to put back into perspective what has become distorted.

John F. McDermott, M.D.
Director, Inpatient Service
Children's Psychiatric Hospital
University of Michigan